A People in Focus Book

STEPHEN HAWKING

Unlocking the Universe

Sheridan Simon

dP|DILLON PRESS, INC.
Minneapolis, Minnesota 55415

Acknowledgments

A book like this one could not have been written without the kind assistance of others, each one a busy professional who took time out to help me provide readers with the clearest possible picture of the life and work of Stephen Hawking. Dr. Robert Berman, who was Hawking's tutor at Oxford, provided me with valuable insights into his college career. S. C. Wilkinson, Headmaster of Saint Albans School, sent me some unpublished material about Stephen Hawking's public school days.

I also wish to acknowledge photographs kindly provided to me by the Royal Greenwich Observatory, by The Master and Fellows of University College, Oxford, and by Angelique Wheelock and Rose Simon. Additional photographs were supplied by Manni Mason's Pictures, Globe Photos/Homer Sykes, Kalmbach Publishing Co./Odyssey magazine, and the National Aeronautics and Space Administration.

Library of Congress Cataloging-in-Publication Data

Simon, Sheridan.
    Unlocking the universe : a biography of Stephen Hawking / Sheridan Simon.
        p.   cm. (A People in focus book)
    Includes bibliographical references and index.
    Summary: Examines the education, research, and personal life of the renowned British theoretical physicist who has taken the study of cosmology farther than most in his field, despite his need for wheelchair and computer in order to travel and communicate.
    ISBN 0-87518-455-3 (lib. bdg.):
    1. Hawking, S. W. (Stephen W.)—Juvenile literature.   2. Physicists—Great Britain—Biography—Juvenile literature. [1. Hawking, S. W. (Stephen W.)   2. Physicists.   3. Physically handicapped.]   I. Title.   II. Series.
QC16.H33S55   1991
530'.092—dc20
[B]
[92]   90-40849
                                                                              CIP
                                                                              AC

Dillon Press, Inc., 242 Portland Avenue South
Minneapolis, Minnesota 55415

Printed in the United States of America
1 2 3 4 5 6 7 8 9 10 00 99 98 97 96 95 94 93 92 91

Contents

Chapter/One

Into a Black Hole

Eight thousand light years from Earth, a star is dying.

The dying star is magnificent. A hundred thousand times brighter than the Sun and thirty times as big, its blue-white light shines across the vast distance that separates it from our own familiar planet. It has lived for perhaps a million years. It would have lived for another million if not for the strange companion that is eating it. But day by day, year by year, the companion tears away the hot gases that make up the blue-white giant and swallows them.

The companion is called Cygnus X-1. It is very small, only a few miles across, but its hunger is without limit. Tiny, but incredibly dense, Cygnus X-1 is so tightly packed that its city-sized body

This is an artist's view of what Cygnus X-1 might look like as its incredible gravitational pull sucks matter from the surface of a nearby star.

weighs more than six times as much as our Sun. So much mass in such a small region produces a gigantic gravitational force. It is this force that reaches out millions of miles to rip away the gases that make up the body of its doomed neighbor.

As great clouds of gas from the blue-white star are pulled into Cygnus X-1, they are squeezed into a volume only a few miles across. This squeezing heats the gas to a temperature of millions of degrees. The gas is so hot that it radiates a storm of X rays out into space.

Cygnus X-1 is not the only one of its kind in the Universe. Others are known as well. They are called black holes.

Only miles across, but many times heavier than the Sun, a black hole produces such a great gravitational force that it can "eat" nearby stars. Yet this is only one of its powers.

A black hole's gravity can reach far into space to capture objects moving at thousands of miles per second—faster than any spaceship ever built. A black hole's gravity is so powerful that not even light—moving at 186,282 miles per second—can escape from it. The X-ray glare from the gases squeezed into Cygnus X-1 and others like it comes from an area more than a hundred miles away from the center of the black hole.

Closer in, a few miles from the center, nothing at all can escape. There is only darkness, and a strange warping of the Universe. Time itself becomes twisted until the direction of the black hole's center points the way toward the future. An object can no more escape its fall toward the center of a black hole than you can turn and walk backward into the past.

Few human beings can study and understand black holes. Those few specialists who can bring new knowledge about black holes into the world are called theoretical physicists. They are people of great talent and imagination. Perhaps the greatest of them is Stephen Hawking.

At first glance, Hawking seems very ordinary. He has medium length, light brown hair, and wears glasses with rather large, squarish lenses. His ears stick out and are somewhat pointed, fitting well with the wide mouth that is often curled into an elfin grin. Serious scientist though he is, Hawking is known for his excellent sense of humor.

Many people might expect Hawking to wear a white lab coat, like scientists in movies. Others would guess that a famous scientist would dress in a three-piece suit with a tie. But Stephen Hawking's clothing fits his personality. His feet are usually covered by boots. He wears baggy pants, a

striped shirt, and a rumpled, wool sports coat.

No matter what he is wearing, though, Hawking can almost always be found sitting in a high-backed red leather seat. It is the seat of an electric wheelchair. His eyes twinkle with humor and interest. His very active mind is filled with incredible knowledge about the Universe. Yet his body never moves. He has been confined to a wheelchair since his late twenties. He will never be free of it again.

Stephen Hawking has amyotrophic lateral sclerosis, or ALS, a severe and crippling disease. He cannot walk, stand, or feed himself. He cannot speak or write. He can move his left hand just enough to work the controls of his wheelchair and the computer that is his only means of communication. Yet he has carried the study of black holes farther than any other person.

Exciting as they are, black holes are no longer the focus of Hawking's work in physics. His central interest is cosmology, the study of the origin of the Universe. The mighty mind inside the weakened body has produced new ideas that may bring us to an understanding of questions that humans have pondered for thousands of years. How did the Universe begin? How did it reach its present state? What will happen to it in the future? How will it end—if it ends at all? And what part does God play

Stephen Hawking is one of the foremost physicists of the twentieth century.

in the origin, life, and eventual end of the Universe?

These are questions whose answers may change our whole outlook on the world—not just in physics, but in philosophy and religion as well. The questions have been asked for many centuries. They are so difficult that it is amazing that humans can even think about answering them. Yet we may well see them answered within our lifetimes if Hawking's research is successful.

Hawking is considered the greatest theoretical physicist of the late twentieth century, and one of the greatest in all of human history. And yet, he is more than just a scientist. He is also a writer. His popular book, *A Brief History of Time*, is the best-selling scientific work in history. It has been translated into more than two dozen languages. At England's University of Cambridge, Hawking's wit, good humor, and broad grin make him a favorite among both students and other scientists.

In the minds of many of his fellow scientists, Hawking's name stands beside those of Newton and Einstein. These brilliant earlier physicists forever changed human understanding of the Universe. In both his personal and professional life, Stephen Hawking has dealt with some of the greatest challenges a person can face. This is his story.

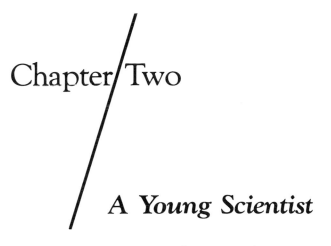

Chapter/Two

A *Young Scientist*

Stephen William Hawking was born on January 8, 1942, in the university town of Oxford, England. His parents had lived in London, but the British capital was heavily bombed by the Nazi air force during World War II. The Hawkings thought Oxford would be a much safer place for the birth of their first child.

Both of Stephen's parents had graduated from world famous University of Oxford. They expected their children to work hard and get a good education, too. Because the Hawkings thought reading and learning were important, books were a big part of their children's lives.

Stephen was the oldest of four children. He was a healthy, active boy who showed no signs of the disease that would strike him in his early twenties. He also showed no signs of his later genius. His work in school was no better than average, and he was rather slow in learning to read.

Stephen was unusual in one way, though, even when he was very young. He liked to take apart clocks and radios. He was curious about the way the parts fit together, and how they moved. "I always wanted to know how everything worked," he said. "I would take things apart...but they didn't often go back together."

His tinkering was fun for him, but it also helped show him what he wanted to do with his life. By the time he was eight or nine years old, Stephen knew that he wanted to be a scientist when he grew up.

Stephen's father, Dr. Frank Hawking, was both a medical doctor and a scientist. He had graduated from Oxford's University College in 1927 with First Class Honors in animal physiology. Scientists in this field study the way cells, tissues, and organs work. Frank Hawking won several scholarships and prizes while in college, and went on to become a doctor in 1933.

In 1947, when Stephen was five years old, Frank Hawking worked at Britain's National Institute for Medical Research. In time, he became head of the Division of Parasitology. There, he studied tropical diseases such as sleeping sickness.

Having a scientist for a father must have been an important influence on young Stephen. Even so, the younger Hawking was never very interested in biology himself. Stephen once said that "the biological sciences werc...too hazy for me."

Although Stephen was born in Oxford, he grew up mainly in London and Saint Albans, a small town twenty miles northwest of the British capital. Stephen's parents sent him to Saint Albans School when he was eleven years old.

This is a public school, like those attended by many British children. A British public school is different from an American public school, though. In the United States, Saint Albans would be called a "private school" because it charges tuition.

The competition at Saint Albans was challenging even for the boy who would one day be considered one of the greatest geniuses of the twentieth century. "I was never more than half way up the class at school," he admits with a smile.

Stephen's class was a very talented one, though. Harry Schofield was one of Stephen's math teachers at the school. He remembers that the dozen or so students in Stephen's class all won scholarships to Oxford and Cambridge, the two best universities in England. "Stephen didn't stand out against them,"

An aerial view of Saint Albans School in the 1950s.

Schofield remembers, "though they did stand out among the rest of the school."

Mr. Schofield remembers one of Stephen's habits, even after more than thirty years. "One thing I remember about his schoolwork is how untidy it was—full of ink blots!"

Stephen tells a story about this time of his life. "When I was twelve, one of my friends bet another friend a bag of sweets [candy] that I would never come to anything. I don't know if this bet was ever settled, and, if so, which way it was decided."

Michael Church was one of Stephen's classmates at Saint Albans School. He remembers Stephen as a "classroom clown." He also says that some of the other students sometimes teased Stephen in the showers. Because Stephen was underweight and unathletic at this age, he was not very successful at sports. This was as much a problem for a boy in the 1950s as it is for a boy in the 1990s. "Being skinny and uncoordinated," Church remembers, "he was a dead loss at games except for cross-country runs, where weightlessness coupled with will was an advantage." Even as a boy, Stephen had plenty of determination.

Stephen's interest in science became real excitement when he first began to study chemistry. His eagerness and impatience, combined with his poor coordination, caused some disasters in the laboratory. Church recalls Stephen "with three fuming test tubes wedged between the fingers of his right hand, picking up a pen with the same hand to write down his findings..."

In the 1950s, students at Saint Albans School were required to take part in military-style drills wearing uniforms like those worn by the British army. Parades in uniform were held on Fridays, and students were expected to be neat. With his large glasses, untidy hair, and ink on his collar,

The science block of Saint Albans School.

Stephen always stood out among the marchers.

Stephen had a strange way of talking as a young boy. It was as if he was impatient to get his ideas out. He was in such a hurry to express himself that he did not form all his words correctly. Other students joked about this, and claimed that he spoke not English, but "Hawkingese."

As a child, Stephen had enjoyed taking things apart to see how they worked. During his years at Saint Albans School, he learned to build things as well. Many of his fellow classmates enjoyed building model airplanes. Stephen, though, wanted his to be radio controlled. Today, radio-controlled model planes can be bought in stores, but in the 1950s, electronic toys and other items were almost unknown. Stephen designed his own electrical circuits and built them, along with the plane itself. His first plane was odd-looking, with pieces of balsa wood sticking out through glued-on tissue paper. The model plane was not very pretty—but it worked!

Encouraged by his success, Stephen went on to design and build radio-controlled boats and tanks. These worked even better than the plane had. He was still not a mechanical or electronic genius, though. His Saint Albans classmate, Michael Church, remembers that Stephen once took apart an old television set to get the vacuum tubes he needed to build an amplifier. Stephen managed to give himself a 500-volt shock in the process.

As if radio-controlled planes, boats, and tanks were not enough, Stephen even set out to build a computer—in 1958! Since there were only a few computers in the whole world at that time, the project was extremely challenging. Stephen and several other members of Saint Albans School's Mathematical Society used parts from an old telephone switchboard. Articles about the students' computer appeared in a number of British newspapers.

Stephen and his friends called the computer LUCE, which stood for Logical Uniselector Computing Engine. The school newspaper, the *Albanian*, published an article about LUCE in May 1958. The article said that "this machine answers some fairly useless though quite complex logical problems." In pre-computer days, students used clumsy devices called slide rules to do calculations. The writer of the article in the *Albanian* also joked that some day every student would have a computer like LUCE in his or her pocket. Although this was science fiction in 1958, today most students do use calculators.

Despite Stephen's success in designing and building "high tech" devices, his greatest talent at school was mathematics. One of his friends remembers just how good Stephen was. "He had incredible...insight. While I would be worrying away at a complicated problem, he just *knew* the answer—he didn't have to think about it."

Like most boys his age, Stephen enjoyed playing games. Often, though, he was more interested in inventing the rules for new games than in playing old ones. He made up one called the Feudal Game, based on events in the history of England. Stephen used a map of England as it was in the Middle Ages as a game board. He included correct

Students study at the School Memorial Library at Saint Albans.

family trees of important historical figures, armies, laws, and government officials. It sounds much like some of our modern role-playing games. But his friends complained that the game took too long to play. One throw of the dice sometimes led to such complicated situations that a whole evening was used up figuring out one "move."

In addition to his many other activities, Stephen tried acting. In 1959, he played the part of Cinna in Shakespeare's *Julius Caesar*. The play tells the story of the murder of Julius Caesar and the civil war that followed. An article about the play appeared in the *Albanian*. It stated that "few who were there will ever forget the cry of triumph which Cinna (S.W. Hawking) produced to herald the rebirth of liberty." The line Stephen shouted follows the stabbing of Caesar in Act II, Scene 1, of the play: "Liberty! Freedom! Tyranny is dead! Run hence, proclaim, cry it about the streets."

Stephen's interest in science continued. He began concentrating on what would become his specialty. By the time Stephen was fourteen, he knew that he wanted to be either a physicist or a mathematician. Mathematicians study symbols such as numbers, and the rules that they follow under different circumstances. Physicists, on the other hand, use mathematical symbols to study real things such as matter and energy, and how they interact. Today, this kind of ambition in a teenager is impressive. But Stephen's father tried to discourage him. He wanted his son to have a career in another area, such as medicine, Frank Hawking's own specialty.

In 1956, when Stephen was fourteen, there was not much demand for physicists. The first artificial satellite, *Sputnik I*, did not orbit the Earth until a year later. There was not a home computer, or even a calculator, in the whole world. No one knew about the future explosive growth of high technology in the 1970s, 1980s, and 1990s. Frank Hawking was concerned that his son was not being realistic about his future. He worried that, as a physicist or mathematician, Stephen would never be able to find a good job.

Scientific research lies at the leading edge of society's advances. One branch of literature that describes science and its impact on society is science fiction.

Like many scientists, Stephen enjoyed reading science fiction as a teenager. A common theme of science fiction in the late 1950s was extrasensory perception, or ESP. Many stories dealt with telepathy (mind reading), precognition (predicting the future), teleportation (moving oneself by mind power), and telekinesis (moving objects with one's mind). These were fascinating ideas for a young person interested in science.

During the 1950s, genuine scientists conducted experiments involving ESP. The experiments seemed to suggest that some people could slightly influence the numbers that came up on thrown dice. The experiments were not very convincing because the results could not be repeated. But they caused a lot of publicity.

Stephen was curious about the concept of ESP. When he was fifteen, he carried out a series of dice-throwing experiments to see if he could find any evidence of ESP. The results of his tests were negative. Stephen became convinced that ESP did not exist. "Whenever the experiments got results," he said, "the experiment...was faulty. Whenever the experimental techniques were sound, the results were no good."

Considering the excitement surrounding ESP at the time, Stephen's results show excellent discipline in a young scientist. Science is exciting. It can be very easy at times to get carried away and see evidence when there is none. This is a real danger in all areas of science. It is one reason why careful scientists always check and recheck their discoveries before announcing them—and why other scientists then repeat the checking.

Hawking is not impressed by people who believe in ESP today. "People taking it seriously are at the stage where I was when I was a teenager," he says. ESP is a fine topic for science fiction, he believes, but should not be confused with scientific truth.

Still, Hawking realizes that the sense of wonder found in science fiction stories has influenced his work. Creativity and imagination play an important role in both science and storytelling. With his typical humor, Hawking once said that "I read a fair amount of science fiction in my teens. Now I write it, only I like to think of it as science fact."

In his free time at Saint Albans, Stephen devoted a lot of time to reading, playing, and performing experiments of his own. He never worked very hard in school, though, and his grades were a disappointment to his parents. They were eager to have Stephen study at the University of Oxford. Frank Hawking brought his son with him several times to visit Professor Robert Berman, a physicist at Oxford's University College.

Stephen wanted to go to Oxford as well, but his parents worried that he would not be accepted. His work in high school was so average that they thought he would fail the university's difficult entrance exam.

Stephen pleasantly surprised his parents by getting a nearly perfect score on the physics portion of his exam. Later, he was so impressive during his interview at the university that he was accepted despite his high school grades. In 1959, at the age of seventeen, Stephen moved to Oxford to begin attending classes there.

Chapter/Three

College at Oxford

"I Stephen William Hawking from St. Albans School, born on 8 January 1942 son of Frank Hawking of St. Albans Hertfordshire herewith enter my name in the College Register

S.W. Hawking"

So reads Stephen's entry in the University College Book of Admissions, signed by every student admitted to the college. The handwriting is sloppy, a word is messily crossed out, and Stephen left out the period at the end of the sentence. Even though he had almost missed the chance to go to Oxford, Stephen did not change his bad habits once there.

Stephen's career at Oxford was not much like that of students at American universities. In the United States, students usually take a variety of courses, with tests and final exams in each course. A student who passes enough courses receives a diploma. Usually, a student spends four years in college in the United States before graduating.

The British university system works differently, and Oxford's system is a good example. For sports and for social purposes, Oxford is divided into about thirty colleges. University College, where Stephen studied, is the oldest of these, founded in 1249. Oxford as a whole provides lectures, classes, and labs for students studying each topic, such as physics. The university makes no effort to ensure that students are keeping up with their studies, though. This responsibility lies with the Fellows (professors) at the individual colleges.

Each college has at least one Fellow in all of the major subject areas. The Fellow arranges small group meetings, called tutorials, where students are required to produce written work. The small groups are run by teachers called tutors. It is a tutor's job to make sure that students do enough work to pass the two very difficult "public examinations" at the end of the three years of study. A student must pass the public examinations to

Oxford is one of the oldest and most respected universities in England.

graduate, so a tutor's job is a very important one. Stephen was lucky enough to have Professor Robert Berman, a talented physicist and teacher, as his tutor.

When Stephen entered Oxford in 1959, he found that many of the other students were a good deal older than he was. They had entered the university after spending several years in the army. Stephen remembers the attitude of most of his fellow students as "very casual, very antiwork." They did not take their studies seriously, and encouraged Stephen to be lazy as well. Many of his fellow students actually resented those who studied hard.

Possibly because of this poor attitude, the requirements in first-year physics at Oxford were not very strict when Stephen arrived. As a result, he did not find physics challenging enough. Instead, he spent his first year reading, or majoring in, mathematics. He later changed his mind, reading physics during his last two years. Another talented young student, Gordon Berry, followed the same route. Dr. Berry is now a well-known research physicist at Argonne National Laboratory near Chicago.

Stephen was popular with his fellow students because of his good humor. He kept his hair a bit long while he was in college, even though this style did not become common until the Beatles became popular a few years later. Stephen read science fiction, as he had in high school, but did not spend much time on his studies.

At Oxford Stephen also took an interest in athletics. He became involved in rowing, a popular sport at British universities. Several different types of boats, called racing shells, are involved in this sport. The colleges at Oxford compete against each other in rowing. There are rivalries between some colleges that go back more than a hundred years. In fact, the first recorded race between eight-man shells took place at Oxford in 1815.

Stephen raced in eight-man shells on the University College team, as his father had before him. The lighter the weight carried by a shell, the faster it can go. Stephen weighed only 140 pounds when he entered Oxford. He was a coxswain, which meant he steered the racing shell.

Despite his outside interests and lack of serious effort, Stephen did very well at physics. His tutor, Robert Berman, recalls that, "he did very little work, really, because anything that was doable, he could do. It was only necessary for him to know that something could be done, and he could do it without looking to see how other people did it."

Professor Berman says that, although Stephen

did not spend much time on his problems, he always completed them. Sometimes, however, Stephen tossed his completed work into Professor Berman's wastebasket before leaving class. Some of the other physics students were horrified to see this, Professor Berman recalls. Stephen threw away work, he said, "that they would have framed on the wall if they could have done it in a year!"

This does not mean that Stephen's classmates were not intelligent. Today, one of these students, Karl A. Gehring, directs high-temperature superconductor research at General Electric. Another, Jonathon W. Hodby, is a Fellow of Balliol College at Oxford.

Stephen did not toss out his work to show off. According to Professor Berman, "He didn't push his cleverness; there was no need." He also had no need to save his work for future reference. Once he had figured out how to solve a particular problem, he did not need to keep his paper to remind himself later of how he had done it. He did not keep notes or buy physics books, either. In fact, some people who knew him at the time guessed that Stephen's main interest in physics books was finding mistakes in them!

For most people, physics is a very challenging field of study. Nearly everyone—even the best students—must struggle to master it. Physics involves the use of calculus and vector analysis, branches of mathematics that are difficult to understand. Students usually spend a long time working through difficult calculations to solve homework or exam problems. They sometimes end up throwing away work that took hours to do after finding a small mistake made near the beginning.

Despite the frustrations, most physicists think that all the effort is worthwhile. The discoveries that are made are always interesting, often surprising, and sometimes incredibly beautiful. Relationships can be found between events that seem at first to be quite different from one another. For example, physics allows people to make a connection between the rocking of tree limbs in the wind and the slow pulsations of supergiant stars. Physicists also find relationships that bind our everyday experiences to events occurring in distant galaxies.

The ordinary physics student requires much time and effort to solve problems. Yet Stephen Hawking did not seem to suffer these frustrations. Even as a young college student, the work came easily to him. "Undergraduate physics was simply not a challenge for him," said Berman. "He could do any problem put before him without even trying."

Hawking himself remembers how little work

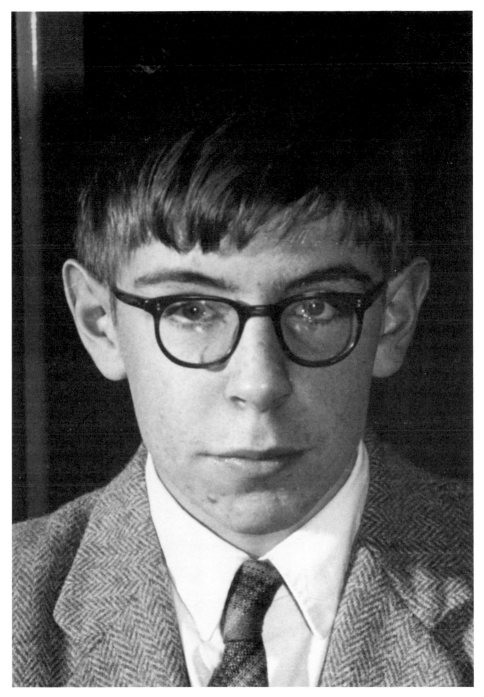

Stephen Hawking at eighteen years of age, shortly after he began his studies at Oxford.

he put into his studies. He once estimated that he did only about one thousand hours of work during his three years at Oxford. This amounts to an average of only an hour a day. Most physics students spend ten hours or more a day on their homework.

During his second year at Oxford, Stephen decided he wanted to be a theoretical physicist. The study of physics can be divided into two fields—theoretical and experimental. Experimental physicists are the people who carry out measurements and make observations. They determine the basic properties of objects or systems of objects, such as their temperatures, speeds, electrical charges, or masses. Experimentalists are the people who use complicated equipment such as particle accelerators, radio telescopes, and high-intensity lasers.

Theoreticians attempt to find patterns in the data discovered by the experimentalists. These patterns of behavior allow theoreticians to understand the processes being studied, and to make predictions of future experimental results. Both kinds of physics are necessary in order to get a complete understanding of the Universe around us. Each field needs the other. But the talents and background needed for each are quite different.

At Oxford Stephen worked in several areas of physics and astronomy. During a summer course in

The Royal Greenwich Observatory, where Stephen Hawking worked with Sir Richard Woolley, a noted British astronomer.

astronomy, he had the good fortune to work with the Astronomer Royal of Great Britain, Sir Richard Woolley, at the Royal Greenwich Observatory. Woolley was studying a double star—a pair of suns circling each other as they travel together through space.

Despite the talent and reputation of the instructor and the excellent telescope, Stephen was not impressed. The two suns looked like nothing more than blurred and fuzzy dots to him. They were not nearly as exciting as some of his theoretical physics discoveries had been. This experience left Stephen more determined than ever to continue his career in theoretical physics.

When the end of his years at Oxford drew near, Stephen decided to continue his studies in physics. He would graduate with a bachelor's degree, but wanted to go on to earn a doctorate, or Ph.D., in physics, specializing in cosmology. Cosmology is the study of the origin, evolution, and future of the Universe. One of the world centers for the study of cosmology is at the University of Cambridge, Oxford's ancient rival. Stephen was determined to study there.

To earn a scholarship to do his doctoral research at Cambridge, Stephen needed to graduate from Oxford with First Class Honors. In the United States, the very best graduates are awarded their degrees *summa cum laude* (with highest honors). Students ranking just below this level are awarded their degrees *magna cum laude* (with high honors). In Britain, the best students are awarded their degrees with First Class Honors followed by Second Class Honors. In other words, to get into Cambridge, Stephen needed to be at the very top of his class.

But Stephen's outstanding ability in physics was weakened by his bad study habits. After three years at Oxford, Stephen's final exam scores left him on the borderline between First and Second Class Honors. In order to determine how to award his degree, the Oxford faculty decided to give him an oral examination. Stephen would have to stand before a panel of professors and answer their questions aloud. An oral exam is difficult to prepare for and quite stressful. A professor usually has much more knowledge about the subject than a student because of the professor's many years of experience.

While Stephen was preparing for his exam, Professor Berman went to see Dr. Batchelor, head of Cambridge's physics department. Professor Berman asked about Stephen's chances of getting into Cambridge. According to Batchelor, twenty scholarships were available, and twenty-four First Class Honors students had already applied. Despite this, Berman convinced the head of the department to hold one scholarship until Stephen's exam results were known. "I don't imagine that they regretted that decision," says Professor Berman.

Stephen did not seem to be nervous about the exam. When one of the examiners asked him about his future plans, he said, "If I get a First [Class Honors], I shall go to Cambridge. If I get a Second [Class Honors], I will remain at Oxford. So I expect you will give me a First." Stephen's lazy attitude and sloppy appearance had not impressed his professors at Oxford. As a result, he assumed they would be glad to see him leave.

Stephen's performance during the exam was amazing. His tutor, Robert Berman, remembers the event well. ''The examiners were...intelligent enough to realize they were talking to someone far cleverer than most of themselves.''

Stephen received an almost perfect grade on the test. He graduated from Oxford with the First Class Honors he had wanted.

As he prepared to leave Oxford, Stephen's only worries were physical ones. He noticed that his movements were becoming clumsy. He would even become slightly paralyzed at times. It became difficult for him to tie his shoes, and sometimes to talk.

But pushing these problems aside, Stephen entered the doctoral program in theoretical physics at the University of Cambridge in 1962. Hawking was only twenty years old, and his future in science seemed very bright.

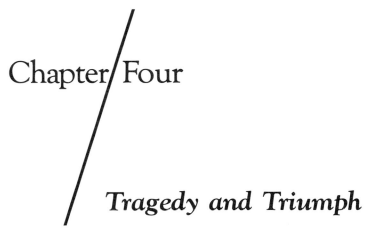

Chapter Four

Tragedy and Triumph

As he entered Cambridge, Stephen was ready to begin serious work. He was self-confident, and had every reason to be. Despite his poor study habits at Oxford, he knew that he was an outstanding physics student. His unusual ability was recognized by his professors as well. His tutor at Cambridge was to be Dennis Sciama, a well-known expert in the study of Einstein's theory of general relativity.

Stephen was now ready to tackle the biggest mystery of all. His interest in cosmology meant that he would try to find answers to questions that had been asked for centuries: How did the Universe begin? How did it get to be the way it is today? How will it end—or will it end at all?

Theoretical physicists try to answer these

Saint John's College at the University of Cambridge.

questions by analyzing the data collected by experimental physicists. The experimentalists must perform a great number of experiments and observations. They use many advanced instruments and computers.

Fortunately for Stephen, he was more interested in the theoretical side of physics. By its very nature, experimental work requires building, repairing, and setting up equipment. "I was lucky to have chosen work in theoretical physics," he said, "because that was one of the few areas in which my condition would not be a serious handicap."

Hawking had seen the first signs of his disease during his last year at Oxford. At first, they did not concern him. But after he entered Cambridge, the symptoms grew more severe. Alarmed, he entered a hospital for some tests.

The results of the tests were grim. Stephen was told that he had amyotrophic lateral sclerosis, or ALS. In the United States, ALS is more commonly called Lou Gehrig's disease, in honor of the New York Yankee's baseball superstar who died of it in 1941.

ALS is a disease which slowly destroys the nerves in the brain and the spine that control the muscles. Its first symptoms usually involve muscular twitching of the hands, and slurred speech or difficulty in swallowing. The disease is painless, and has no effect on thinking or memory. People with ALS can hear, feel, see, taste, and smell perfectly well. In a sense, this makes ALS all the more difficult for those who have it. They remain fully aware of what is happening to their bodies, yet they have no control over them. ALS is usually fatal because it eventually destroys the muscles used in breathing. This leads to pneumonia or suffocation.

Most of those with ALS die within a year or two of their first symptoms. Very few live more than five years with the disease, and almost none more than ten. When Stephen was diagnosed as having ALS in 1962, he was given these facts and told he had two years to live.

At the time he learned he had ALS, Stephen was twenty-one years old—young, brilliant, and with every hope of a long and successful career. The idea that he had only two years to live nearly destroyed Hawking. Certain that he was facing death, Stephen stopped working on his study of cosmology. Deeply depressed, he sat alone in his room day after day. There, he would listen to classical music by the German composer Wagner and read science fiction books.

"The doctors offered no cure or assurance that it would not get worse," Hawking remembers. "At first, the disease seemed to progress fairly rapidly. There did not seem to be much point in working on my research because I didn't expect to live long enough to finish my Ph.D."

During this period, one of Stephen's strongest supporters was his father. As a doctor, Frank Hawking knew about ALS, its symptoms, and its treatments. He was not happy with the treatment his son was receiving. After researching ALS further, Frank Hawking prepared a mixture of steroids and vitamins for Stephen to help strengthen his weakened and decaying muscles.

Frank Hawking also talked with Dennis Sciama, Stephen's tutor. Dr. Hawking asked Sciama to help Stephen finish his doctoral work early, so he could at least have the satisfaction of getting his Ph.D. before he died. But Sciama rejected the appeal.

After almost two years of depression and the constant threat of death, Stephen's condition stopped getting worse. Although he would never be healthy again, it became clear that he was in no immediate danger. He was not yet confined to a wheelchair, and though weak, he was not yet badly disabled.

Once his depression lifted slightly, Stephen realized that his mind was not affected by ALS. His memory and reasoning ability worked just as well as before the disease. He was still able to continue his research in theoretical physics, and pursue his greatest interest—cosmology. Stephen's spirits lifted. He had finally found a way to live with his disability. After this, he began to take real pleasure in life again. "When you are faced with the possibility of an early death," he once said, "it makes one realize that life is worth living and that there are lots of things you want to do."

Stephen's life was greatly changed by ALS,

and not just in physical terms. His whole attitude became different. Before he learned that he had ALS, he was active and intelligent, but wasted a lot of time. "Before my condition was diagnosed, I had been very bored with life," he said. He knew what he was interested in, and liked doing it. But he put little effort into his studies, working only a few hours a week. The years of his life seemed to stretch endlessly before him; there was no need to rush things. But after he found out he had ALS, his life looked much too short. If he was to learn all he wished to learn, he had to become far more focused than he had been. Once Stephen knew he had no time to waste, he decided to make the best use he could of the time he had left.

Hawking remembers the period he spent in the hospital after his first symptoms worried him. A boy in the bed opposite from him died of leukemia, a type of cancer, while Stephen was there. The pain and suffering of the boy have always stayed in his memory. "Whenever I feel inclined to be sorry for myself," he says, "I remember that boy."

After he regained his spirits, Stephen found that there were many things he wanted to do. One was to get married. On New Year's Day of 1963, soon after he discovered he had ALS, he met Jane Wilde at a party in Saint Albans. Three years younger than Stephen, Jane was a language student about to enter Westfield College of the University of London. Stephen was immediately attracted by this energetic young woman with brown hair and sparkling blue eyes. She, in turn, liked "his wit and questioning intelligence." Although he seemed very self-confident, she remembers that "there was something lost. He knew something was happening to him of which he wasn't in control." Jane was right. He was struggling to come to terms with the idea that he could die very soon.

In 1964, once Stephen had begun to recover from his depression, he and Jane became engaged. His new responsibilities to Jane seemed to help Stephen focus attention on his life rather than his death. He began once again to take his career seriously. "If I were to get married, I had to get a job," he said. "And to get a job, I had to finish my Ph.D. I therefore started working hard for the first time in my life. To my surprise, I found that I liked it."

Stephen and Jane were married in 1965. In speaking of his marriage, Hawking said, "It made me determined to live, to go on. Jane really gave me the will to live."

During the first year of their marriage, Jane commuted every week between London and Cambridge, a sixty-mile trip, while she finished her graduate work. The Hawkings had some trouble finding a suitable place to live in Cambridge. It was becoming difficult for Stephen to get around on his own. He had asked his college for help in his search, but he was told that the college did not help graduate students find housing.

Although Jane was very busy, she typed Stephen's doctoral dissertation, a long research report required for a Ph.D. Stephen completed the dissertation, called *Properties of the Expanding Universe*, and received his doctorate in 1966. His great research into cosmology had begun.

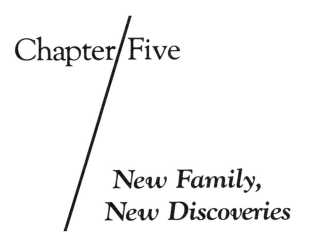

Chapter Five

New Family, New Discoveries

The five years from 1965 to 1970 were busy ones for Stephen and Jane in more ways than one. Stephen's work in theoretical physics drew attention from other researchers around the world. And on the personal side, the Hawkings became a family. Their son Robert was born in 1967, and their daughter Lucy in 1970. Stephen had the delights and distractions of two babies in his home while he tried to work.

Eventually, Cambridge agreed to give the Hawkings a home, in which Stephen still lives today. The ground-floor apartment is in a large, old house with big rooms and wide doors. This arrangement makes it easier for Stephen to get around. The house is surrounded by a lawn and garden that are

The Hawking home at 5 West Road in Cambridge.

tended by the college gardening staff.

Many burdens began to fall on Jane during this time. Although he could still walk—with difficulty—it was becoming harder and harder for Stephen to care for himself. As his muscles became steadily weaker, he began to have trouble feeding himself, let alone little Robert and the baby, Lucy. Stephen was not able to help much with household chores such as cooking, shopping, and cleaning.

Jane accepted all the responsibilities that fell to her without complaint. "I didn't really know what to expect when we got married," she once said in an interview. "I think Stephen had felt very depressed and I wanted to find some purpose to my existence...and I suppose I found it in the idea of looking after him."

After being awarded his Ph.D., Stephen decided to continue his studies of cosmology. Because Cambridge was (and still is) a world center for research in that area, Stephen stayed there instead of seeking a job somewhere else.

Hawking was given several different duties by the university. He was made a Fellow of Gonville and Caius College, and a member of the graduate staff of the Institute for Theoretical Astronomy. In addition, since he was now officially *Dr.* Hawking, he was appointed to the faculty of the Department of Applied Mathematics and Theoretical Physics. He could now add the title *Professor* to his name, as well.

Cambridge's Department of Applied Mathematics and Theoretical Physics is located in a nineteenth century brick building near Cambridge's Silver Street. Silver Street itself is winding and very narrow. It has been described as having room for three horses to walk side by side—a tight fit for a modern car.

The Department of Applied Mathematics and Theoretical Physics is located on an alley off this

Cambridge's Department of Applied Mathematics and Theoretical Physics is located in this nineteenth century brick building.

Stephen Hawking in his office at the Department of Applied Mathematics and Theoretical Physics.

narrow street. The alley leads into a courtyard and parking lot. At one end of the courtyard is a blue door with a glass window and a small brass plate with the department's name on it. This entrance leads into a hallway that twists and turns past a number of closed doors, finally ending in a fairly large commons room with a high ceiling. The commons room is used by department members for both professional and social purposes—a combination lounge and classroom.

Stephen's office is near the commons room. It

was here that he continued his work in cosmology during the late 1960s. Today, Stephen uses a different entrance from most visitors. At the rear of the old brick building is a long ramp, suitable for a motorized wheelchair. Stephen reaches the ramp by passing down another alley. Fortunately, the Department of Applied Mathematics and Theoretical Physics is only a few hundred yards from the Hawking home at 5 West Road.

Although he was distracted by his worsening health and two small children, Stephen was quickly gaining an international reputation for his work. Between 1965 and 1970, Stephen's discoveries in theoretical physics placed him among the most respected researchers in the world.

His studies of the origin of the Universe became more and more involved with new work being done by some of his colleagues at Cambridge. Because of the importance of this new work to cosmology, in the late 1960s Stephen began to study the incredible structures known as black holes.

To understand black holes, begin by imagining yourself tossing a ball straight up into the air. Your hand provides the force that starts the ball upward. But it is the force of gravity that pulls the ball back toward the ground. As gravity pulls on it, the ball moves upward more and more slowly and comes to a stop for an instant. Then it falls back down, moving faster and faster as it approaches the ground. The faster the ball is moving when it leaves your hand, the higher it goes and the longer it takes to fall back.

Now suppose you threw the ball really fast, using something more powerful than your own muscles—a rocket, perhaps. What would happen then?

It turns out that the same pattern holds for rocket launches as for balls thrown with your own muscles. The faster the rocket throws its payload—the ball, for example—upward, the higher the payload travels. And the higher it moves, the longer it takes gravity to pull the payload back to Earth. In fact, it is possible to use a rocket to throw a payload so fast that gravity never brings it to a stop at all. The payload continues to move farther and farther from Earth, never to return.

The speed needed to throw a payload fast enough so that gravity can never pull it back is called *escape speed*. Escape speed from Earth is about 25,000 miles (40,000 kilometers) per hour, or roughly 7 miles (11 kilometers) per second. If you could run this fast, you could circle the Earth's equator in just about an hour.

But Earth's gravity is fairly weak. In our own solar system, there is an object with a much more

powerful gravitational pull: the Sun. If you were to stand on the surface of the Sun, its gravity would pull on you with a force twenty-eight times stronger than Earth's. An average person would weigh as much as a minivan.

With such a strong gravitational force, you might expect that the Sun's escape speed would be a good deal larger than Earth's. It is. Escape speed from the surface of the Sun is nearly 400 miles (640 kilometers) per second, fast enough to zip from Boston to Miami in less time than it takes you to read this sentence.

Although the Sun's gravity and escape speed are a good deal greater than those of Earth, they are weak when compared to a neutron star. These amazing objects are as heavy as the Sun, but only as big as a large city. Packing so much mass into such a small volume makes them extremely dense. If you used the cap of a pen to scoop up some material from the middle of a neutron star, it would hold a mass as great as that of all the people who have ever lived on Earth. Looked at another way, all the buildings in the United States would have to be squeezed into that pen cap to produce a density as great as that in the centers of neutron stars.

With their matter packed so tightly, neutron stars have enormously powerful gravity. At the sur-

---

The escape speed for the Apollo spacecraft launched from Earth is 25,000 miles (40,000 kilometers) per hour.

face of a neutron star, you would weigh as much as a mountain, squashed by a pull 10 billion times stronger than Earth's. And to reach the escape speed of a neutron star, you would have to travel at tens of thousands of miles per second. That is fast enough to fly from the Earth to the Moon in just a few seconds.

But there are places in the Universe where matter has been compressed even more tightly. These objects have gravitational pulls even stronger than those of neutron stars. Their gravity is so strong that no known force can resist it. It squeezes these objects, crushes them, and collapses them until they could fit in a room, in a pocket, even inside a pinhead. They collapse until they have no size at all!

These tiny but immensely massive objects are called singularities. Their gravitational pull is so strong that it is impossible for nearby objects to escape. Close to a singularity, the escape speed is greater than the speed of light, the fastest speed that anything can move. Nothing, not even a ray of light, can escape from the region around a singularity. For this reason, in 1969 the American cosmologist John A. Wheeler gave the region near a singularity a descriptive name: a black hole.

The surface dividing the black hole from the

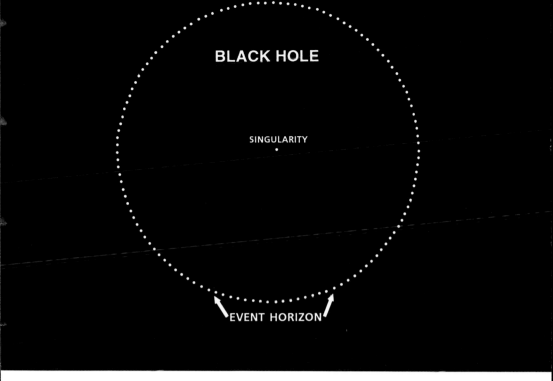

BLACK HOLE

SINGULARITY

EVENT HORIZON

This diagram shows a black hole surrounding a singularity in space, and the event horizon at the edge of the black hole.

rest of the Universe is called the "event horizon." Any events happening inside it can never be seen from outside, since not even light can pass out of a black hole. Whatever happens inside the event horizon remains unseen, much like events taking place over the horizon here on Earth.

The concept of black holes had been known for quite a while in theoretical physics. But the serious study of these amazing objects really began in the early 1960s, while Stephen was doing his Ph.D. research at Cambridge. Earlier, physicists had thought of singularities as an interesting idea.

Still, no one believed that such objects actually existed. Singularities seemed to be objects that were very heavy—possibly much heavier than the Sun—but they had *zero* size! Objects such as neutron stars were strange enough, with sun-sized masses packed into city-sized objects. Packing mass into a region with zero size was just too hard for physicists to believe. Many were convinced that there was no way for such strange objects to be formed in the real Universe.

But in 1965, Stephen Hawking read an important paper by Roger Penrose, a British mathematician and physicist at Cambridge. In his paper, Penrose proved that if an object such as a neutron star collapsed, a singularity with a black hole around it would almost always be formed. This proof was the first strong indication to physicists that such weird objects as black holes might actually exist. No one yet had any idea of where—or even how—to look for black holes. Yet Penrose's paper produced much excitement among theoretical physicists.

One of the excited scientists was Stephen Hawking. When Stephen read about Penrose's discovery in 1965, he soon realized something important. Think of how the collapse of a neutron star and the formation of a singularity would look as a movie. If the movie were run in reverse, a singularity would seem to burst outward. It would expand as fast as the neutron star collapsed.

Penrose had shown that the collapse of a star could lead to the formation of a singularity. Hawking guessed that a much more important event had started with a singularity. In this case, it exploded outward in the reverse of Penrose's collapse. This event was the Big Bang—the birth of the Universe.

Chapter/Six

The Birth of the Universe

In the 1930s astronomers discovered that the Universe is expanding. This discovery surprised physicists. Even Albert Einstein, the physicist who developed the theory of relativity, was amazed. No one had ever imagined that the entire Universe could be growing larger. But the evidence is strong. Stars form huge groups called galaxies, each one containing many billions of stars. With the help of large telescopes, astronomers have studied millions of galaxies very far from our own. All of these are rushing apart, each getting ever farther from its neighbors.

Since the Universe is steadily expanding, in the past it must have been smaller. Long ago, everything was closer together. The farther back

Albert Einstein developed the theory of relativity early in the twentieth century.

into the past we look, the smaller the Universe must have been. Scientists think that this expansion began about 15 billion years ago. At this time, the entire Universe was very close together—much like a singularity, in fact. It has been expanding at high speed ever since.

The rapid expansion of the Universe must have started in an extremely violent explosion. In that ancient explosion, all of the material we see around us today was thrown apart at enormous speed. Physicists call this tremendous explosion the Big Bang.

For five years, Hawking and Penrose worked together to find out if the Universe itself had started with the explosion of a singularity.

Stephen and his colleagues wanted to know the answers to many questions. Was the Big Bang the origin of the Universe, or did the Universe exist in some other form before this explosion? Will the expansion of the Universe ever come to a stop? If it does, what happens afterward?

Physicists now know that the answers to these questions are linked together. Both the origin and future of the Universe depend a lot on how massive it is. The bigger the mass of the Universe—the heavier it is—the greater its gravitational force. This force of gravity tries to pull the galaxies together even as they are flying apart, just as Earth's gravity slows down a stone that is thrown upward.

The gravitational pull gradually slows the outward movement of the galaxies. If the mass of the Universe is too small, this pull will not be strong enough to completely stop the galaxies from moving apart. But if there is enough mass, the expansion will slow down and eventually end. After that, the long expansion will be replaced by an equally long contraction, or inward movement. Gravity will pull the galaxies closer together, as they were billions of years ago. The Universe will collapse

In this diagram, the Universe begins with the Big Bang, expands for billions of years, and ends in the Big Crunch. This is a theory developed by cosmologists.

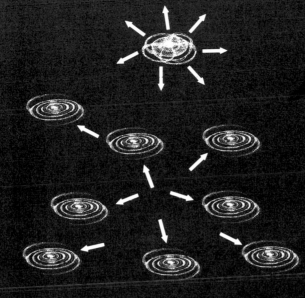

DISTANT PAST
The Big Bang

PRESENT DAY
Expansion of universe
continues as galaxies
rush apart

DISTANT FUTURE
Mutual gravitational
attraction of galaxies
halts expansion

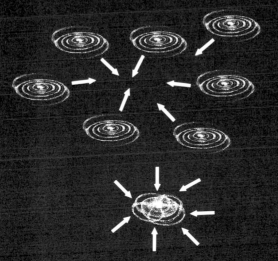

MORE DISTANT FUTURE
Mutual gravitational
attraction of galaxies
contracts universe

**STILL MORE
DISTANT FUTURE**
The Big Crunch

under the force of its own enormous gravity.

Physicists call this event the Big Crunch. They believe that if it occurs, it will closely resemble the collapse of a neutron star into a singularity. This process was first described by Roger Penrose in the 1965 paper that inspired Stephen Hawking to begin his own study of black holes.

Despite his increasing disabilities, Hawking worked hard with Penrose. In 1970 they thought they had found mathematical proof for Stephen's theory. If the mass of the Universe is too small to halt its growth, they said, then it must have begun as a singularity. Just as a collapsing neutron star has a singularity in its future, a universe that will expand forever has a singularity in its past.

But Stephen discovered a flaw in his own argument. Stephen had used Einstein's theory of general relativity to calculate gravity's effect on the Universe's mass. Einstein's theory was first published in 1915. Since then it has worked well to describe large and small gravitational effects, both inside and outside the Solar System. But all of the experiments and observations done in testing general relativity have involved long distances, such as those separating the Sun and planets. This means that general relativity may not be the right way to understand the gravitational forces produced by very small objects such as atoms or singularities.

The Universe has a huge mass. But in its earliest instants, just after the Big Bang, the Universe was even smaller than an atom! This was the problem with the theory invented by Hawking and Penrose. They could not be sure that they had correctly predicted the effects of gravity on the tiny Universe during the first few instants of its existence.

Fortunately, the properties of very small particles had been studied by physicists before Stephen's work on cosmology began. To understand the behavior of tiny systems such as atoms, physicists developed the theory of quantum mechanics in the 1930s. Quantum mechanics explains the behavior of atoms and even smaller objects such as electrons and protons. For example, most of modern electronics is based on calculations done using quantum mechanics.

General relativity works well only for large-scale calculations. Quantum mechanics, on the other hand, works well only on a small scale. Until Stephen Hawking came along, no one had ever combined the talent, hard work, and creativity needed to use both theories to solve important problems. In the early 1970s, Hawking worked with the two theories to learn more about the behavior of black holes, singularities, and the origin of the Universe.

In 1971, shortly after Stephen had begun to combine general relativity with quantum mechanics, the study of black holes took an important turn. Early research on black holes had been based entirely on theories. Scientists were not certain that their ideas were correct. Until Penrose's work in 1965, astronomers had not tried hard to find these objects. To begin with, most physicists did not believe they really existed. Also, it looked as if it would be impossible to spot a tiny object that gave off no light, far away in the blackness of space.

But in the late 1960s, theoreticians suggested a way that a black hole might be spotted. If it happened to be located near a normal star, the gravity of the star and the black hole would hold them close together. They would swing around each other like a pair of dancers. Although astronomers could not see the black hole itself, they might be able to spot the normal companion star. It would look as if the companion star were moving in an orbit around an empty point in space—the location of the black hole.

If an ordinary star were located very close to a black hole, a more dramatic effect was expected. The black hole's strong gravity would pull material off the surface of the normal star. The material would whirl into the black hole in a spiral-shaped path. It would look much like a hurricane, with the black hole located where the storm's eye would be. As the hot gas was squeezed inward by the black hole's gravity, it would get hotter and hotter. Its temperature would rise to millions of degrees in the last few instants before it was squeezed through the event horizon. The super-hot gas would send out a storm of X rays.

Astronomers agreed that if they found a normal star moving in an orbit around nothing, they might have found a black hole. But if there was also a dazzling production of X rays coming from the system, it seemed nearly certain that a black hole would be present.

In 1971 an American satellite called Uhuru was launched into orbit. It was equipped to spot astronomical sources of X rays. These cannot be observed by Earth-based instruments, since X rays are absorbed by Earth's atmosphere long before they can reach the ground. Uhuru was aimed at several systems that looked like single stars moving in orbits around empty space—space that might be the location of a black hole. In one of these systems, Uhuru spotted a source of X rays which was later named Cygnus X-1.

For a time, astronomers were not sure if the invisible companion of the bright blue star in

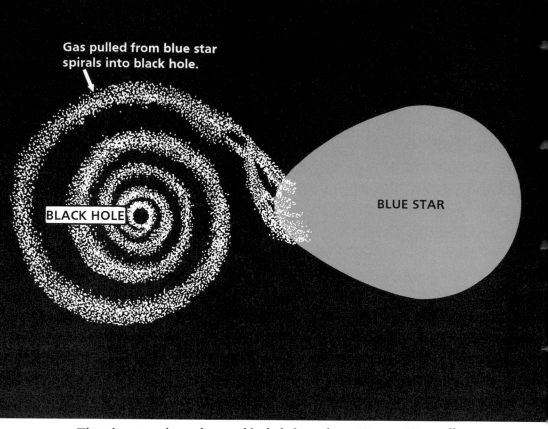

Gas pulled from blue star spirals into black hole.

BLACK HOLE

BLUE STAR

This drawing shows how a black hole such as Cygnus X-1 pulls material off the surface of a nearby star.

Cygnus X-1 was really a black hole. In 1975, Stephen made a bet about Cygnus X-1 with American physicist Kip Thorne. Surprisingly, Stephen bet his friend that Cygnus X-1 was not a black hole! He described this bet as "insurance." If Cygnus X-1 turned out not to be a black hole, Stephen would at least win his bet—a four-year subscription to the British magazine *Private Eye.*

As of 1990, astronomers worldwide generally believe that Cygnus X-1 does include a black hole. If so, Stephen has lost his bet.

The discovery of Cygnus X-1 convinced many astronomers that black holes actually existed. It seemed that they could be formed by the collapse of a fairly ordinary neutron star, as shown by Penrose. But Stephen soon suggested another possibility. In the incredibly violent explosion of the Big Bang, tremendous pressures would have been created. Such pressures would have been strong enough to crush some of the exploding gases into singularities. Stephen referred to these objects formed during the Big Bang as "primordial [earliest] black holes."

While he was developing his theory of primordial black holes, Stephen's physical condition grew slowly but steadily worse. By 1972, he needed to use a wheelchair to get around. The loss of his ability to walk was very difficult for him. Yet Stephen faced each new burden with courage. He continued his research about black holes and made important contributions in theoretical physics.

Theoreticians had always believed that a black hole could only grow bigger and more massive as time went on. Every bit of matter that fell through the event horizon was lost forever, they thought. Nothing could move fast enough to escape from the gravity of the central singularity once it had fallen into the black hole itself.

Hawking, though, found evidence that black

holes might not always grow larger. In fact, he found that they could actually disappear completely over long periods of time.

This theory had an odd beginning. In 1970, not long after the birth of his daughter Lucy, Stephen had an important insight one night while preparing for bed. "My disability made this a rather slow process, so I had plenty of time," he said. Since he was growing quite weak, getting ready for bed took him much longer than it would take most people. Stephen used this time to think about black holes. Since his ALS had been discovered, he tried to make the best use of every available minute.

That night, he began thinking about the giant gravitational field around a singularity. The gravitational field of a black hole contains so much energy, Stephen thought, that strange things could happen. For example, gravitational energy could create tiny, charged particles called electrons and positrons. These particles are always created in pairs, and most of the time disappear almost immediately. The electron and positron destroy each other and change back into gravitational energy.

On rare occasions, Stephen realized, one of the two particles could fall through the event horizon of the black hole before destroying its partner. The particle left outside the black hole might—under just the right conditions—escape into space.

According to Hawking's theory, a black hole might gradually dissolve as its gravitational energy turned into electrons and positrons that escaped outward into space. Smaller, less massive black holes would evaporate faster than their bigger relatives. A large black hole would evaporate slowly at first, then faster and faster as it became smaller and smaller. At the end, the last bit of the original object would vanish in a blinding explosion.

Stephen was so surprised by his discovery that he waited for three years before sharing his ideas with other physicists. His first suggestion was made at an informal seminar held at the University of Oxford in November of that year.

After the scientific discussion at this meeting, Stephen's colleagues shook their heads sadly. Hawking had done good work in the past, they felt, but this strange new theory simply could not be true. Despite their lack of support, Stephen Hawking had faith in his theory. As it turned out, he was right. His work was about to change the world's understanding of black holes.

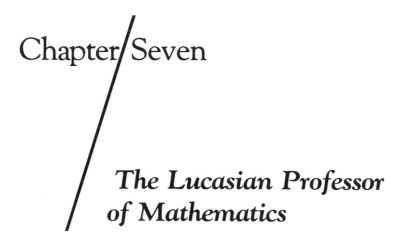

Chapter Seven

The Lucasian Professor of Mathematics

The results of the meeting at Oxford were not encouraging, yet Stephen pressed forward. Perhaps he was prompted to share his ideas about black hole evaporation by the 1973 publication of his first book. In *The Large-Scale Structure of Space-Time*, Hawking and his colleague George F. R. Ellis summed up some of Stephen's new theories.

His theory about the evaporation of black holes involved the use of both general relativity and quantum mechanics. This combination, known as quantum gravity, made many of Hawking's colleagues uncomfortable. They knew that the two theories did not fit together well. As a result, they were not at all sure that Stephen was right.

On March 1, 1974, Hawking published a paper

on his new work in the highly respected British scientific journal *Nature*. He did not describe black holes as dead black objects giving off no energy. Instead, Stephen's calculations suggested that small black holes would be blazing sources of radiation as they dissolved. Primordial black holes, formed in the first instants after the Big Bang, could be exploding often enough to be detected by astronomers. The paper astonished many theoretical physicists with its surprising conclusions.

In the winter of 1974, Hawking finally presented a formal paper entitled "Black Hole Explosions?" The question mark is some indication of how unsure Stephen himself was of his own results. The paper was read for him at the Rutherford-Appleton Laboratory, a major British research center west of London. The other physicists at the conference listened politely to his talk. Still, at the end of Hawking's lecture, most of them could not accept his new results. John Taylor, a mathematics professor at the University of London, summed up the feelings of many of those present: "Sorry, Stephen, but this is absolute rubbish."

Despite this criticism, Hawking had not lost the respect of his colleagues. As his work was checked more carefully over the next few years, his ideas about the evaporation of black holes eventually were accepted by other physicists.

In the spring of 1974, shortly after the Ruther-ford-Appleton meeting, Hawking traveled from Cambridge to London. In a stately old mansion, near London's lovely St. James Park, Stephen Hawking became a member of the Royal Society of Great Britain. For three hundred years the Royal Society has included as its members the best of British scientists. Only thirty-two years old, Hawking was one of the youngest people ever to be made a member.

Physically so weak that he had to be carried up the steps into the building, Stephen could not walk up to the stage to sign the Royal Society's roll book. Instead, the Society's president, Sir Alan Hodgkin, brought the book down from the stage to Stephen, who sat beside Jane in the audience. Slowly, painfully, Stephen Hawking signed the book that holds the names of some of the greatest physicists in history. One of these is Isaac Newton, who first developed the theory of gravity that served as a foundation for Stephen's own work.

During the next few years, Hawking received many honors and awards. Later in 1974, he was named Fairchild Distinguished Scholar at the California Institute of Technology, better known as Cal Tech. The following year he was awarded the

Eddington Medal by the Royal Astronomical Society of Great Britain. He also won the Pius XI Gold Medal from the Pontifical Academy of Sciences. Located in the Vatican in Rome, the Pontifical Academy is part of the Roman Catholic Church.

In addition to these awards from other organizations, Stephen received an honor from the University of Cambridge. In 1975, he received a two-year appointment as Reader in Gravitational Physics. Hawking's genius was becoming widely recognized across the world.

By this time, though, Stephen could no longer feed himself. He also needed help getting into and out of bed. With Jane's assistance, he managed for a long time to cope with day to day living. For many years Jane was able to take care of Stephen and their children. She tried to provide a happy and stable home for the family.

Like her husband, Jane earned a Ph.D.—hers in modern languages. While teaching French and Spanish at a Cambridge high school, Jane helped Stephen to enjoy life as much as possible. The Hawkings were familiar figures at concerts and plays in Cambridge. At the Cambridge Arts Theatre, the staff removed one of the seats to leave a place for his wheelchair.

As Stephen continued his research into black

holes and cosmology, he received more praise from scientists and scientific organizations across the world. Cambridge promoted him to the post of Professor of Gravitational Physics. Soon people outside the world of physics began to notice him, too. In January 1977, he and his work were described in an issue of *Newsweek,* a major American news magazine.

In 1978, Hawking was given yet another great honor when he received the Albert Einstein Award for Theoretical Physics. Some people found this surprising because Hawking's discoveries conflicted with Einstein's in some ways. Decades earlier, Einstein had complained about quantum mechanics. This was the branch of physics Stephen used to learn how gravitational energy could be transformed into tiny particles. Einstein had not liked the fact that quantum mechanics never makes definite predictions. Instead, it indicates probabilities, or odds. In this way it is like a local weather forecaster predicting a 50 percent chance of rain.

Einstein, on the other hand, thought of the Universe as having a few specific rules that exactly determined the behavior of physical systems. "God does not play dice with the Universe," he said in 1932. Forty-five years later, Stephen's work with the quantum mechanical properties of the singularities

Stephen and Jane Hawking at home with their three children: Robert (left), *Lucy* (center), *and Timothy* (right).

lurking inside black holes caused him to correct Einstein. "God not only throws dice," Hawking said, "but sometimes throws them where they cannot be seen."

Stephen's family was growing along with his collection of awards. In 1979, the Hawkings' youngest child, Timothy, was born. By this time, Robert was twelve, and Lucy was nine. The older children could now help Jane take care of the new infant.

In that same year, there were other important events in Stephen's life. Stephen and his friend

Werner Israel edited a book about the progress made in understanding gravity. The book was called *General Relativity: An Einstein Centenary Survey.*

On April 29, 1979, Stephen was given one of the highest honors of his career. He was named Lucasian Professor of Mathematics by the University of Cambridge. This post has been held by some of the greatest of British scientists, including Nobel Prize winners such as Paul Dirac. But the most famous person ever to hold that position was the world's first great authority on gravity, Isaac Newton.

It is customary for the scientist named Lucasian Professor to deliver a special lecture. By this time, though, Stephen's speech had been seriously affected by the advancing ALS. The lecture was delivered for him by one of his students. Its title was "Is the End in Sight for Theoretical Physics?"

In this talk, Hawking suggested that all of the most basic properties of the Universe might be understood by physicists within a fairly short time. In fact, he predicted that this could happen by the end of the twentieth century. While there would still be important questions to be dealt with by scientists, claimed Hawking, the basic nature of the forces controlling the Universe would soon be understood. Most physicists, though, did not agree with the new Lucasian Professor. Only someone with Hawking's outstanding reputation would have dared to make such a bold prediction—he had been right too many times before.

As the years passed, Stephen had less and less control over his muscles. Eventually he needed help even in eating and drinking. In 1980 he and Jane hired a series of community and private nurses. The nurses helped Stephen for an hour or two in the morning and evening. By this time his speech had become very difficult to understand. He was no longer able to control his throat, lips, and tongue well enough to form easily recognizable words.

Fortunately, his colleagues and students at Cambridge were used to his way of speaking. They could still understand him, and he was able to give lectures by relaying his words through one of his friends. His sense of humor and brilliant insights into physics remained intact. Cambridge physics students always considered a Hawking lecture to be a real treat.

By the early 1980s, Hawking was a very popular figure, in high demand by students and scientists worldwide. Still, he found time to do new research. He and his colleague M. Rocek edited a book filled with articles about ways in which quantum mechanics and general relativity could be combined. The book was called *Superspace and Supergravity.*

In 1981 Stephen went to Moscow for a conference on quantum gravity. After the conclusion of
the conference, Hawking himself gave a special seminar on some problems with theoretical studies of
the very early Universe. The seminar must have
been difficult to follow for the other scientists present. Stephen's own words could no longer be understood except by those who heard him on a daily
basis, such as his family and students. So Stephen
spoke—slowly and with difficulty—and his words
were repeated in clearer English by one of his graduate students. Since many of the scientists present at
the Moscow conference spoke Russian, those who
did not know English needed a second translation.

In 1981 Hawking was also awarded an honorary
degree by the University of Chicago. Some say that
after the ceremony, he went with a group of colleagues to a Chicago disco. There, according to this
story, he drove his wheelchair out onto the dance
floor and spun it in dizzy circles.

This kind of behavior is typical of him. In 1981
Stephen was thirty-nine years old, permanently
confined to a wheelchair, and barely able to communicate with his friends, students, and loved ones.
But with Jane's help he was never forced to give in
to his physical problems. Stephen has firm opinions
about this: "My advice to other disabled people is,

concentrate on those things that you can do, and for which your disability is not a handicap. Above all, avoid making a profession of being disabled, with a permanent chip on your shoulder."

By the end of 1981, Hawking was ready to return to his original love—cosmology. His interest in this area was renewed at a special conference on the origin of the Universe organized by Jesuit scholars at the Vatican in Rome.

The following year began very well for Hawking. In addition to several more awards and honors from British and American organizations, he was named Commander of the British Empire by Queen Elizabeth II. This is one of the highest honors awarded in Great Britain.

Despite all of the praise and attention, Stephen still did not feel he had accomplished all he could. Awards, no matter how much prestige they carry, belong to the narrow limits of our own small planet. Stephen's ambitions extend much farther in both space and time. "My goal is simple," he said. "It is the complete understanding of the Universe."

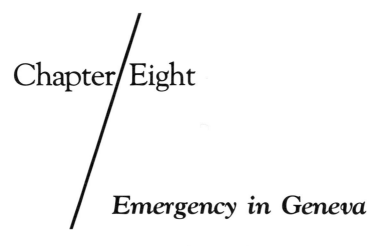

Chapter / Eight

Emergency in Geneva

In 1983, Stephen Hawking and his colleague James Hartle achieved an important goal. They developed a different model for the origin and evolution of the Universe.

For many years Hawking and his coworkers had believed that the Big Bang began with the explosion of a singularity. But singularities are a real problem to theoretical physicists. To begin with, a singularity has zero size. Any calculations involving singularities always lead to problems similar to dividing by zero. In mathematical terms, dividing by zero is undefined. Try it on your calculator to see what happens.

Because of this problem, the laws of physics can't be used to understand the histories of singularities themselves. If the Universe started as a singularity, there is no way that theoretical physics can reach further into the past than the singularity. By its very nature, the singularity does not obey the laws of physics that we know. As a result, its behavior cannot be predicted or even understood. The failure of singularities to obey the laws of physics concerned Stephen and many of his colleagues.

The new theory developed by Hawking and Hartle claimed that the Universe did not begin with the explosion of a singularity. Instead, their new view indicated that the Universe could pass smoothly through a stage of very small—but not zero—size. It would then expand rapidly in a Big Bang. Galaxies would move farther and farther apart for many billions of years. But eventually the pull of gravity would slow the expansion, halt it, and cause the Universe to begin shrinking. Billions of years later, the Universe would collapse in what cosmologists call the Big Crunch. For a moment the entire Universe would occupy a very small region, but the region would not be as small as a singularity. From this tiny, compressed state, the Universe would emerge again into a Big Bang.

In 1984, Hawking and Hartle worked to develop their new theory further. Despite his ever-worsening condition, Stephen seemed able to overcome every weakness to continue his search for an understanding of the Universe. The following year, he finished a first draft of A *Brief History of Time.*

But on a visit to Geneva, Switzerland, Stephen developed pneumonia. Pneumonia is an infection of the lungs and breathing passages. This disease is a serious problem for people with ALS. ALS causes the muscles that help in breathing to weaken and break down. When ALS victims get an illness such as pneumonia, they find it nearly impossible to breathe. Pneumonia is the cause of death for many ALS victims.

Choking, unable to breathe, Stephen's life was in immediate danger. The Swiss doctors were forced to perform a tracheotomy, which removed part of Stephen's trachea. The trachea is the tube that connects the breathing passages of the nose and throat with the lungs. By opening a passage through his throat, the surgeons were able to provide a path for air to reach his lungs.

By the time Jane arrived at the Geneva hospital, Stephen was on a life support system in an intensive care unit. The Swiss doctors were amazed that a man as ill as Stephen was making trips across Europe. In fact, Stephen has visited the United States more than thirty times. He has also traveled to Moscow at least seven times, and has run his powered wheelchair atop the Great Wall of China. Stephen and Jane always tried as hard as possible to keep his disability from limiting his activities.

Stephen's life was saved by the doctors in Geneva. But the bout with pneumonia had weakened his already frail body. When he returned home, Jane was unable to care for him alone.

Stephen now needed full-time nursing care. For the first time in their marriage, Jane was not completely responsible for keeping Stephen alive. Bringing in a team of medical personnel was certainly necessary to preserve Stephen's fragile health. But Stephen was deeply affected by the new situation.

Jane once commented on the need for full-time care. "Everybody thought it was a realistic step," she said. "But for him it was a step downwards. He felt that he was giving in to his condition. There were so many instances when a practical step for everybody else meant, for him, giving in—an admission of defeat. I suppose that's what kept him going. Some people would call it determination, some obstinacy [stubbornness]—I've called it both at one time or another."

Although he might feel that he has taken

some backward steps, Stephen Hawking still insists on living his life as fully as possible. The medical team now travels with Stephen and his assistants when he makes trips abroad.

Stephen's own view of himself is quite different from that of other people. "I suppose that I would be described as a severely disabled person, but that is not how I see myself. Rather, I see myself as a scientist who happens to be disabled, just as I might happen to be color blind. Most people are disabled or disadvantaged in some way. I may be a bit more disabled than many, but it is just in physical ways that can be helped by other people and by equipment like my wheelchair and computer. I have been very lucky that my disability has not prevented me from doing what I really want to do, which is physics."

Despite Stephen's courage, the tracheotomy in 1985 was a heavy blow. The trachea also provides a path for air to pass through the larynx, or voice box. The operation that saved his life destroyed Stephen's ability to talk at all. Now even the slow and slurred speech he had had before was impossible for him. As a final tragedy, the operation also cost Stephen his sense of smell.

For a time after the operation, Stephen could communicate only with great difficulty. A person could point at letters of the alphabet on a sheet of paper. Stephen would respond by raising his eyebrows when the right letter was indicated. Carrying on any kind of conversation was extremely hard under these circumstances. Writing scientific papers—the means by which physicists communicate their discoveries to each other—was almost impossible. The energetic, creative mind of Stephen Hawking seemed trapped within his failing body, unable to communicate his ideas.

At this difficult time, modern technology came to Stephen's rescue. Walt Woltosz, a computer software specialist at Words Plus, Inc., of Sunnyvale, California, heard about Stephen's problem. He sent Stephen a copy of a program he had written called Living Center. The program runs on small computers like the one attached to Stephen's electric wheelchair. It provides him with lists of words.

Fortunately, Stephen could still move his fingers slightly. By applying light pressure on a switch under one hand, he could choose the words he wished to use from the list, or go on to other lists. The program included about 2,600 words. In addition, the computer was connected to a voice synthesizing device that spoke the words Stephen chose. The computer and speech synthesizer were mounted on Stephen's chair by his associate, David Mason.

Woltosz's program and the computer hardware it runs provide Hawking with a voice. The lines of communication between him and his fellow human beings are open again. A fairly short time ago—even as recently as 1980—the hardware that gives Stephen his voice did not exist. High technology, an offspring of twentieth-century physics, is now helping one of the world's great physicists in a very personal way. It is also benefitting the rest of the world by giving access to the thoughts and ideas of a first-class mind.

Even so, communicating in this way is difficult. Because he needs to choose each word from a list, Stephen's speech is quite slow, only about six words per minute. Ordinary conversation takes place at about two hundred words per minute. That is nearly three dozen times faster than Stephen's synthesized voice.

Many people would find this situation depressing. But Hawking is a man of unusual courage. "If you are disabled physically, you cannot afford to be disabled psychologically," he says. He has adjusted to this situation as he has to so many others in the past, with a mixture of acceptance and good humor. He apologizes to interviewers because his speech synthesizer (programmed in California) has an American accent.

Stephen Hawking on the Caius College grounds at the University of Cambridge.

Although Stephen needs help from others in many ways, he can control his electric wheelchair with the movement he still has left in his fingers. When leaving his University of Cambridge office in the evening, he often takes off at high speed down the dark paths that run between his office and his home. To keep up, his nurses and assistants must trot along behind him. The wheelchair can move as fast as a person can run, and Stephen enjoys high-speed travel. He has often zoomed across a busy street, trusting oncoming cars to stop for him—which they do.

Hawking has continued to be honored by organizations across the world. In 1986 he was made a member of the Pontifical Academy of Sciences, a part of the Vatican. In the following year he was named an honorary Doctor of Science by Newcastle University and won the Paul Dirac Medal and Prize from the American Institute of Physics. That year, he and his friend Werner Israel edited another book, *300 Years of Gravitation*. In 1989 Hawking was named Companion of Honor by Queen Elizabeth II, won the Britannica Award, and was named an honorary Doctor of Science by the University of Cambridge.

Despite his physical weakness, Hawking continues to communicate his ideas to professional

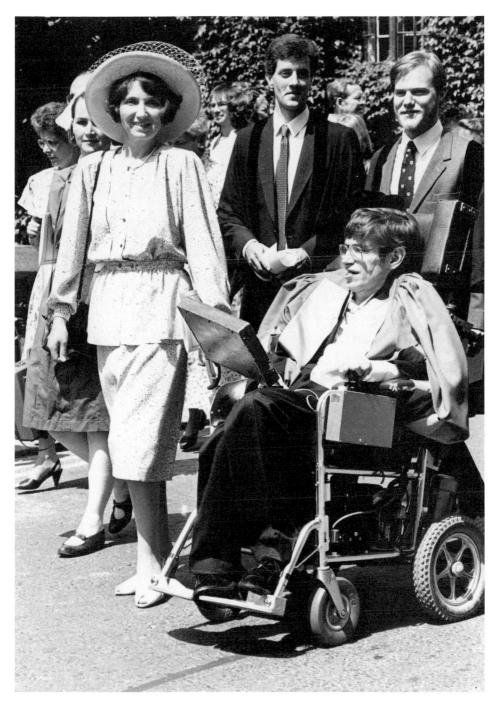

Stephen and Jane Hawking and their son Robert at an honorary degree ceremony.

physicists, college students, and the general public. As recently as 1988, Stephen taught a popular course at Cambridge called "A Short History of the Universe." Every Thursday morning he left his office in the Department of Applied Mathematics and Theoretical Physics for the building where his lecture was to be given. His fast-moving wheelchair led a short parade of two research assistants, a nurse, and usually a journalist or two. Hawking lectured to a packed audience of three hundred people, including undergraduates, graduate students, his nurses, and a few members of the general public. His French-Canadian assistant, Raymond Laflamme, helped him by showing slides. Hawking always included funny quips and jokes in his lectures, which were greeted by much laughter from his audience. The audience enjoyed the lectures thoroughly. Each one ended in a storm of applause—a fine tribute to any teacher.

Before his close call with pneumonia in 1985, Stephen had finished a first draft of *A Brief History of Time*. After he had recovered some strength, he started revising the text with the help of his student Brian Whitt. The book was published in 1988.

For his new book, Hawking chose a publisher of popular nonfiction. He had written many articles on his work for the specialized audience of theoretical physicists. Still, he felt that it was important to communicate the excitement of his new discoveries to the general public as well. "My original aim was to write a book that would sell on airport bookstalls," he once joked.

A Brief History of Time proved to be popular worldwide. Soon after its publication, it appeared on the *New York Times* best-seller list. It replaced a book about astrology—the unscientific study of the influence of heavenly bodies on human affairs. Stephen had decided as a teenager that ESP did not exist. He was delighted by the victory of his book over the other one, because he believed that astrology was no more scientific than ESP. "Cosmology has finally beaten out astrology," he said with pride.

Hawking has very little patience with those who say science includes areas such as astrology and Eastern mysticism. "I think that is a copout," he said in 1988. "People find physics too difficult and so they make out that it's part of some vague, imprecise whole." He is most annoyed when physicists themselves try to find links between physics and what Stephen considers complete nonsense. "Eastern mysticism is an illusion. A physicist who attempts to link it to his own work has abandoned physics."

On the other hand, when asked if he thought physics and art shared a single root, Hawking had a more positive reply. "I don't think they are all that separate. They both try to satisfy our basic yearnings by different means. I look for excellence in both." Perhaps that last sentence shows why Stephen has driven himself so hard to understand the origin of the Universe. He is unwilling to accept second-rate work from others, and certainly not from himself, whether the work is art or science.

Chapter/Nine

Searching for the Ultimate Truths

Stephen Hawking's life and work have taken him a long way from his boyhood and first scientific experiments at Saint Alban's School. His research into black holes has greatly improved our understanding of these incredible objects. But his most important work, cosmology, is still incomplete.

Still, there are some suggestions in his work that might soon lead to the answers to questions that have been with humankind for thousands of years. One of these questions involves both science and religion: Was the Universe created by God?

Earlier in the twentieth century, it seemed clear—as it had to our distant ancestors—that one event could not be explained by natural forces alone: the origin of the Universe. It seemed that

the Universe must have been created by an act of
a Supreme Being operating outside all the laws of
physics. Many, and possibly all, properties of the
Universe could be understood in scientific terms.
Yet the creation of the Universe lay completely
outside the bounds of science. God still had a
place at the very beginning of time and space. "So
long as the Universe had a beginning," said Stephen Hawking in *A Brief History of Time*, "we
could suppose it had a creator."

Hawking's work in the early 1970s seemed to
prove that there was a creator—a Being outside of
all scientific laws and human understanding. At
that time Hawking and Penrose thought they had
proven that the Universe had a singularity in its
past. The origin of the Universe in the explosion
of a singularity does not resemble the creation
stories accepted by Christians, Jews, or Muslims.
Yet it seemed that the properties of the singularity
could not be explained or understood in scientific
terms. That gave it a special meaning. The creation of the Universe still seemed to require the
help of something beyond the laws of the Universe itself.

But as Stephen Hawking continues his research into quantum gravity, the older picture he
helped develop almost twenty years ago is chang-

ing. The effects of quantum gravity seem to suggest that there was not a singularity in the distant past. They also suggest that there will not be one in the distant future. The Universe may not have had its origin in the explosion of a singularity, and may not end in one, either.

The new theory seems more to Hawking's liking. The fact that singularities were not subject to the laws of physics always disturbed him. "The whole history of science has been the gradual realization that events do not happen [by chance], but that they respect a certain underlying order, which may or may not be divinely inspired."

The picture that is slowly emerging from the latest work of Hawking and his colleagues differs from the old theory. Hawking's latest work suggests that the Universe may evolve smoothly from its "end" into a new "beginning." There are no singularities involved at all. The structure of the Universe remains predictable by the laws of physics throughout its history.

In this new picture suggested by Hawking's research, the Universe has no beginning and no end. It is a complete structure, closing back on itself smoothly in both time and space. Each expansion leads to a new contraction. The Big Bang and the Big Crunch are still in the picture, but they involve no singularities. In time the Big Bang and the Big Crunch may be understood completely in terms of the known laws of physics.

Stephen says that if the new theory is correct, "the Universe is a closed system. We don't need to suppose there's something outside the Universe which is not subject to its laws...the laws of science are sufficient to explain the Universe."

This theory makes many people—including scientists—rather uneasy. If it is correct, the Universe is eternal. If the Universe had no beginning and will have no end, it had no moment of creation—no moment in the distant past when a Supreme Being said, "Let there be light."

Stephen Hawking has made this point himself: "If the Universe is really self-contained, having no boundary or edge, it would have neither beginning nor end: it would simply be. What place, then, for a creator?"

Stephen has been asked such questions by others many times. In every case, he has been careful not to reveal his personal religious beliefs. "The more we examine the Universe, the more we find it...obeys certain well-defined laws that operate in different areas. It seems reasonable to suppose that there might be some underlying principles, so that all laws are part of some bigger law from which all other laws can be derived. I think you can ask that question whether or not you believe in God."

In 1983, a reporter pressed Stephen for a more definite answer. Stephen was asked if he thought his new ideas about the origin of the Universe were similar to the religious knowledge revealed to biblical prophets. His reply was carefully worded. It points out some of the important differences between scientific insights, which come from human minds, and religious ones, which may have a different origin.

Were his insights at all like those of the prophets in the Bible? There was, he said, "a certain similarity, in that there is no prescribed route to follow to arrive at a new idea. You have to make an intuitive [unplanned] leap. But the difference is that once you've made the intuitive leap you have to justify it by filling in the intermediate [in between] steps. In my case, it often happens that I have an idea, but then I try to fill in the intermediate steps and find they don't work, so I have to give it up."

The place of a creator in cosmology clearly concerns Stephen Hawking deeply. He mentions God again and again in *A Brief History of Time*. This concern with the roots of religion is very unusual in a scientific book, but then Stephen Hawking is a very unusual man. His work in cosmology has forced him to think about the relationship between science and religion in ways that scientists have carefully avoided for a long time. Still, he has not yet shared with the rest of the world any conclusions he may have drawn.

What does Stephen Hawking really believe about the place of God in the Universe? Does he think that the very concept of God is out of date, part of the ancient and unscientific past? Hawking leaves no clear statement in any of his writings or in any interviews about his own religious beliefs. Dr. Don Page is an American physicist and a Christian. He lived with the Hawkings for several years while working with Stephen at Cambridge. Page said in an interview that he tried on many occasions to engage Stephen in a discussion of religion. Stephen, though, would not discuss his beliefs. Eventually, Dr. Page stopped asking.

Stephen has not even shared his true beliefs with his wife Jane. "There's one aspect of his thought that I find increasingly upsetting and difficult to live with," she said in an interview in 1987. "It's the feeling that—because everything is reduced to a rational, mathematical formula, that must be the truth. There doesn't seem to be room in the minds of people who are working out these things for other sources of inspiration. You can't actually get an answer out of Stephen regarding philosophy....He's now [creating] a theory in which the Universe [has] no beginning and no end and no need for God at all. What I can't understand is whether—and this is something that in the whole twenty-two years of being married to him that I haven't been able to understand—he is working within the bounds of math and science and saying: 'This is what the theory predicts; if you have other interpretations that's up to you.' Or whether he is saying: 'This is the only concrete evidence we have of anything.' I never get an answer; I find it very upsetting."

Jane herself is an Anglican. (American members of this church are called Episcopalians.) Stephen's refusal to give a definite statement about his religious beliefs disturbs her deeply. "I pronounce my view that there are different ways of approaching it and his mathematical way is only one way—and he just smiles."

Sadly, the difference between their religious outlooks may have been part of the reason that the Hawkings separated in 1990. Though they are reported to be on good terms with one another, they continue to hold two very different views of God.

Mathematics is in some ways the language of physics. The mathematics Stephen uses in gaining his own understanding is not the kind that most students think of as math in school. "People have the mistaken impression that mathematics is just equations," he said in a 1988 interview. "In fact, equations are just the boring part of mathematics. I attempt to see things in terms of geometry."

In part, this approach is necessary since Hawking is unable to write down the detailed equations he would need to use in learning more about quantum gravity. Even though Stephen is physically weak, he can picture extremely complicated geometric pictures within his own mind. This ability has amazed his colleagues. Werner Israel, a highly respected cosmologist, said that "he has an ability to visualize four dimensional geometry that is almost unique."

But despite his geometric skills, and the breathtaking insights they have given him, Stephen himself recognizes the limits of mathematics. "What is there that breathes fire into the equations and makes a universe for them to describe? If I knew that, then I would know everything important."

Stephen's recent work lies in one of the most difficult areas of physics. Even most scientists cannot understand it well, and yet it is deeply important to all the world's people. Will the great majority of those who are not theoretical physicists ever share Stephen's discoveries?

It would be easy for a man as gifted as Stephen Hawking to suppose that only he and a few other scientists could understand cosmology, and thus gain an understanding of the true nature of God. But Stephen has never felt that way. Even if his research is successful, and he comes to understand the nature of the Universe at a deeper level than any reached before, he does not believe this knowledge will be shared only by a group of physicists. "If we do discover a complete theory," he says in *A Brief History of Time*," "it should in time be understandable in broad principle by everyone, not just a few scientists."

Stephen Hawking is a man who has explored the deepest and best-kept secrets of the Universe. He has studied the incredible objects known as black holes, and advanced our understanding of them. He is in some ways the finest example of the human ability to think and analyze. His disability has allowed him to push his mental abilities to their natural limits. His reasoning power may be truly unique in the world today. He seems to be on the verge of understanding the origin, evolution, and fate of the Universe. If he

gains this understanding, "then we shall all, philosophers, scientists, and just ordinary people, be able to take part in the discussion of why it is that we and the Universe exist," he says near the end of *A Brief History of Time.*

The book's next passage gives the faintest glimpse of what may be his own personal beliefs. "If we find the answer to that, it would be the ultimate triumph of human reason—for then we would know the mind of God."

Stephen Hawking's career has been dedicated to searching for the answers to questions that are important to all human beings. They are questions that have been asked throughout human history. His efforts go far beyond what would be necessary to satisfy his own curiosity or provide him with the rewards of fame. In his present condition, in fact, they take time away from his research and drain him of energy.

But Stephen has never been one for self-pity, and does not express it now. Instead, he thinks of himself as very lucky. "I have a lot to be positive about. I have an attractive family, I have been successful in my work, and my book has become a best seller. One couldn't ask for much more." The fact that he is physically weak, Stephen feels, is not very important when measured

The work of Stephen Hawking has forever changed human understanding of the Universe.

against all these sources of joy and satisfaction.

In whatever years remain to him, Hawking will continue his search for the ultimate truths. His frail body is a reminder to all of us that we are mortal. But the mind behind the big glasses and the broad smile reaches outward towards the infinite. The ideas created in Stephen Hawking's mind will be with his descendants, and our own, through all the centuries to come.

Glossary

ALS—amyotrophic lateral sclerosis, a disease that causes the nerves that control muscle movement to grow steadily weaker and weaker

astronomer—a scientist who studies planets, stars, galaxies, and other celestial bodies and forces outside the Earth's atmosphere

atom—a tiny system that contains electrons, protons, and (usually) neutrons; all ordinary matter is made of atoms

Big Bang—the immense explosion approximately 15 billion years ago that started the present expansion of the Universe

Big Crunch—according to theory, the collapse of the Universe in the distant future

black hole—a region in space where gravity is so strong that not even light can escape

cosmology—the study of the origin, evolution, and fate of the Universe

electron—a tiny, negatively charged particle, one of the parts that make up all atoms

escape speed—the speed an object must have to move away from another object forever, despite the pull of gravity

event horizon—the outer boundary of a black hole

galaxy—a huge structure including billions of stars as well as gas and dust clouds; there are billions of galaxies in the Universe

gamma ray—a photon similar to light or an X ray, but even more energetic than an X ray

general relativity—the theory developed by Einstein that describes gravity in terms of the geometric structure of space and time

gravity—the force that pulls any two pieces of matter in the Universe toward each other

light-year—the distance traveled by light, moving at 186,282 miles per second, in one year. It equals 5.85 trillion miles

neutron—a tiny, neutral, uncharged particle found in nearly all atoms

neutron star—a star as much as three times as massive as the Sun but only a few tens of miles across, made entirely of neutrons

photon—the basic element of light; photons have properties in common with both waves and particles

physicist—a scientist who studies matter and energy and interactions between them

positron—a positively charged particle; the anti-particle of the electron

quantum gravity—the combined use of the theories of general relativity and quantum mechanics, used by Stephen Hawking to develop new theories about black holes and the origin of the Universe

quantum mechanics—the branch of physics that deals with very tiny objects such as atoms and their parts

radiation—light and other types of photons, such as X rays, gamma rays, and radio waves

singularity—a mass with zero size and infinite density

Universe—everything that ever has been and will be, including the Earth, Sun, Solar System, Galaxy, and all other galaxies

voice synthesizer—a device including a speaker and computer that produces a humanlike voice

X ray—a photon similar to light but much more energetic

Selected Bibliography

Books

Boslough, John. *Stephen Hawking's Universe*. New York: Avon, 1985.

Hawking, Stephen W. *A Brief History of Time*. New York: Bantam, 1988.

Moritz, Charles, ed. *Current Biography Yearbook 1984*. New York: H. W. Wilson, 1984, 155-158.

Magazines, Journals, and Newspapers

Adler, Jerry et al. "Reading God's Mind." *Newsweek* (June 13, 1988): 56-59.

Boslough, John. "Inside the Mind of a Genius." *Reader's Digest* (February, 1984): 118-123.

Carlson, Cathy. "Brave New Universe: A Visit with Stephen Hawking." *MDA Newsmagazine* (Summer, 1989): 8-11.

Church, Michael. "Games with the Cosmos." *The Independent* (St. Albans, England) (June 6, 1988): 12.

Dolphin, Ric. "Glimpses of God." *Maclean's* (September 19, 1988): 44-47.

Harwood, Michael. "The Universe and Dr. Hawking." *New York Times Magazine* (January 23, 1983): 16-19, 53-59, 64.

Hawking, Stephen W. "The Quantum Mechanics of Black Holes." *Scientific American* (January, 1977): 34-40.

———. "Black Hole Explosions?" *Nature* (March 1, 1974): 30-31.

Jaroff, Leon. "Soaring Across Space and Time." *Time* (September 4, 1978): 56.

———. "Roaming the Cosmos." *Time* (February 8, 1988): 58-60.

"Julius Caesar." *Albanian* (St. Albans School, St. Albans, England) (May, 1959): 17.

"Mathematical Society." *Albanian* (St. Albans School, St. Albans, England) (May, 1958): 308.

Mitton, Simon. "Stephen W. Hawking." *Astronomy* (November, 1979): 28-30.

Morais, Richard C. "Genius Unbound." *Forbes* (March 23, 1987): 142.

Overbye, Dennis. "Out from Under the Cosmic Censor: Stephen Hawking's Black Holes." *Sky and Telescope* (August, 1977): 84-89, 108.

Strong, Morgan. "Playboy Interview: Stephen Hawking." *Playboy* (April, 1990): 63-74.

"Talk of the Town." *New Yorker* (April 18, 1988): 30-31.

Waldrop, M. Mitchell. "The Quantum Wave Function of the Universe." *Science* (December 2, 1988): 1248.

Wrottesley, Catriona. *Review This Weekend* (St. Albans, England) (January 27, 1989): 5.

Interviews and Letters

Berman, Robert. Telephone interview with the author from Cambridge, England, March 6, 1990.

———. Letter to the author from Cambridge, England, March 11, 1990.

Page, Don N. Telephone interview with the author from University of Alberta, Canada, February 15, 1990.

Pryke, Geoffrey E. Letter to the author from St. Albans, England, July 21, 1990.

Wilkinson, S. C. Letter to the author from St. Albans, England, March 5, 1990.

Index